THE CROSS

THE PULPIT OF
GOD'S LOVE

Iain H. Murray

THE BANNER OF TRUTH TRUST

THE BANNER OF TRUTH TRUST
3 Murrayfield Road, Edinburgh EH12 6EL, UK
PO Box 621, Carlisle, PA 17013, USA

*

ISBN-13: 978 0 85151 974 6

*

Typeset in 11/14 pt Adobe Garamond Pro at
The Banner of Truth Trust
Printed in the USA by
VersaPress, Inc.,
East Peoria, IL.

The content of this booklet is taken from
Chapter 4, *The Old Evangelicalism,*
(Edinburgh: The Banner of Truth, 2005).

THE CROSS – THE PULPIT OF GOD'S LOVE

'The cross was a pulpit in which Christ
preached his love to the world.'
AUGUSTINE

'Let us remember that God's glory displays itself more illustriously in the Gospel than in the Law, – and that his invitation is now full of love, but that formerly there was nothing but the greatest terrors . . . The Gospel contains nothing but love, provided it be received by faith.'

John Calvin, *Commentaries on the Epistle of Paul to the Hebrews* (Edinburgh: Calvin Translation Society, 1853), pp. 331–332.

'I was standing on the 10th December 1846, at the end of my father's house, and meditating on that precious word that has brought peace to countless weary ones: "God so loved the world, that he gave his only begotten Son, that whosoever believeth in him should not perish, but have eternal life" (*John* 3:16). I saw that God loved me, for I was one of the world. I saw the proof of his love in the giving of his Son Jesus. I saw that "whosoever" meant anybody and everybody, and therefore me, even me. I saw the result of believing – that I would not perish, but have everlasting life. I was enabled to take God at his word. I saw no one, but Jesus only, all in all in redemption. My burden fell from my back, and I was saved. Yes, saved!'

JOHN MACPHERSON, *Life and Labours of Duncan Matheson: The Scottish Evangelist* (Kilmarnock: Ritchie, n.d.), p. 26.

The atonement is the centre of the Christian faith and of the work of the gospel ministry. The purpose of gospel preaching is to make known what God has done in the cross of Jesus Christ. The evangel *is* 'the preaching of the cross' (*1 Cor.* 1:18). Paul states with an oath that his office as a preacher was for the setting forth of the vicarious sufferings of the Son of God, 'who gave himself a ransom for all, to be testified in due time. Whereunto I am ordained a preacher and an apostle' (*1 Tim.* 2:6–7). Accordingly, he writes to the Corinthians: 'I determined not to know anything among you, save Jesus Christ and him crucified' (*1 Cor.* 2:2); 'I delivered unto you first of all that which also I received, how that Christ died for our sins' (*1 Cor.* 15:3). Paul's hearers in Galatia could be described as people 'before whose eyes Jesus Christ has been evidently set forth, crucified' (*Gal.* 3:1). Such is the supremacy of this message that the apostle invokes the curse of God upon any teaching which would add anything to the completeness of what Christ did when he 'gave himself for our sins'(*Gal.* 1:4, 8–9). As George Smeaton has commented on that curse:

> Were the atonement not the principal matter of the gospel, and the highest exhibition of the united wisdom, love and faithfulness of God, – in a word, the greatest act of God in the universe, – that terrible anathema on its subverters would seem to us something inexplicable, if not intolerable.[1]

Smeaton goes on to characterize the ministry of all the apostles in these words:

[1] George Smeaton, *The Apostles' Doctrine of the Atonement* (Edinburgh: Banner of Truth, 1991), p. 19.

Their symbol was the cross; their boast was the cross: they could not live without it; they could not die without it . . . In preaching such a doctrine they exposed themselves to the loss of reputation, to hardships and peril, to persecution and death. But they held on their way, undeterred and undaunted.[2]

If this was apostolic Christianity then we are bound to examine ourselves as to whether our emphasis corresponds with it. The question is all-important because, if God gives this pre-eminence to the cross, it must follow that where there is hesitancy or uncertainty in preaching the death of Christ, there is bound to be a serious weakening, if not a nullifying, of the chief purpose of the gospel ministry. There is much discussion today about how evangelism may be advanced, but in the midst of all the discussion one finds too little consideration of the question whether the cross constantly holds the same position in our message as it very evidently did in that of the apostles.

There is an additional reason why a re-examination of our priorities is needed. Across the English-speaking world there has been a considerable recovery of the doctrinal beliefs which were prominent in the Puritans and the older evangelicalism. In that school of belief there was no doubt concerning the place given to the death of Christ. 'The cross, I see, is that chiefly which moves the sinner,' said John MacDonald, 'the Apostle of the North'.[3] More fully, Thomas Chalmers wrote:

---

[2] Ibid., pp. 16, 20.

[3] John Kennedy, 'The Apostle of the North': The Life and Labours of Dr MacDonald (London: Nelson, 1866), p. 122.

The doctrine of the atonement, urged affectionately on the acceptance of the people, and held forth as the great stepping stone, by which one and all are welcome to enter into reconciliation and a *new life* (for a fully declared gospel is the very reverse of Antinomianism) I hold to form the main staple of all good and efficient pulpit work.[4]

The men who spoke in this way were commonly men whose preaching was marked by evangelistic passion and the anticipation of success. In contrast, while we are thankful for the doctrinal recovery which has been taking place, it has to be questioned whether we have seen a parallel recovery in gospel preaching. If we prize the beliefs of a former age why should it be that we fall so far short of that earlier generation in the winning of souls? When due acknowledgement is made of divine sovereignty and of the hardness of our times, it may be a dangerous assumption to suppose that our weakness as evangelists has no connection with anything doctrinal. Our understanding of the cross is an area where we hope – over against a shallow evangelism – that we are at our strongest, but that very assumption may add to our danger. And where that danger lies was pointed out by Professor John Murray when he wrote not long before his death:

The passion for missions is quenched when we lose sight of the grandeur of the evangel. . . . It is a fact that many, persuaded as they rightly are of the particularism of

[4] W. Hanna, ed., *The Letters of Thomas Chalmers*, (Edinburgh: Banner of Truth, 2007), p. 329.

the plan of salvation and of its various corollaries, have found it difficult to proclaim the full, free, and unrestricted overture of gospel grace. They have laboured under inhibitions arising from fear that in doing so they would impinge upon the sovereignty of God in his saving purposes and operations. The result is that, though formally assenting to the free offer, they lack freedom in the presentation of its appeal and demand.[5]

This is tantamount to saying that while 'many' hold to the same confession of faith as the men I have quoted, they do not resemble them in the freeness with which they preach the cross. Jonathan Edwards believed it is 'past all contradiction' that Christ 'died to give all an opportunity to be saved',[6] and he urged his hearers, 'Accept of the offered love of him who is the only-begotten Son of God.'[7] Yet it is at this very point that there is now uncertainty in some Reformed circles.

[5] John Murray, 'The Atonement and the Free Offer of the Gospel,' *Collected Writings*, vol. 1, (Edinburgh: Banner of Truth, 1976), pp. 59, 81.

[6] Jonathan Edwards, *Works*, vol. 13, *The 'Miscellanies,'* ed. Thomas A. Schafer (New Haven: Yale University Press, 1994), p. 174. This truth, he adds, 'Calvinists themselves never denied.' A. A. Hodge asserts it in his *Evangelical Theology* (Edinburgh: Banner of Truth, 1976), p. 219.

[7] *Works of Jonathan Edwards*, vol. 2 (Edinburgh: Banner of Truth, 1974), p. 933.

TWO TRUTHS

Uncertainty in preaching Christ and the cross arises, as John Murray pointed out, from the difficulty of relating the Scriptures that speak both in particular and in universal terms. Both are to be found in Scripture, as many passages show:

Scripture teaches a definite atonement: that is to say, Christ died with the purpose of saving those whom the Father had given him — a number not vague or indefinite but sure and certain. Thus he says, 'I lay down my life for the sheep' (*John* 10:15); and Paul directs the elders at Ephesus 'to feed the church of God, which he has purchased with his own blood' (*Acts* 20:28). The effect of the death of Christ is definite, there is a 'purchased' people; his sufferings secured reconciliation and freedom from condemnation for all those whose sins he bore, the same number for whom he was 'made sin' are 'made the righteousness of God in him' (*2 Cor.* 5:21). So those whose place he took become the inheritors of all that he accomplished for them: 'By one offering he hath perfected for ever them that are sanctified' (*Heb.* 10:14; see also *Rom.* 8:32). In the words of the *Westminster Confession* (VIII: 8): 'To all those for whom Christ hath purchased redemption, he doth certainly and effectually apply the same.' William Cowper has stated the same truth memorably in his hymn, 'There is a fountain filled with blood':

> Dear dying Lamb, Thy precious blood
> Shall never lose its power,
> Till all the ransomed Church of God
> Be saved, to sin no more.

But if gospel texts speak of the death of Christ in terms of the particular, there are others which direct us to the universal: the message of the cross is to be presented to all in order that they may believe and be reconciled to God. The same God who 'now commands all men everywhere to repent' (*Acts* 17:30), assures every hearer of his willingness to pardon all who trust in Jesus. His direction to preachers is not that they command repentance in all, but confine the invitation to faith and forgiveness to a few. Rather *both* are to be presented together, 'repentance unto remission of sins should be preached in his name among all nations' (*Luke* 24:47).[8] In other words, the good news of a provided forgiveness is to be as universally proclaimed as is the command to repent:

> Come unto me all you that labour and are heavy laden, and I will give you rest (*Matt.* 11:28).
> Preach the gospel to every creature (*Mark* 16:15).
> This is his commandment that we believe on the name of his Son Jesus Christ (*1 John* 3:23).
> Whosoever will, let him take the water of life freely (*Rev.* 22:17).

---

[8] 'Those who deny the free overture of grace must rob the demand for repentance of its gospel implications. Denial dismembers Jesus' word, "repentance unto remission of sins" and it contradicts the plain import of Paul's "all everywhere".' John Murray, *Collected Writings,* vol. 1, p. 60. In translating 'unto remission', Murray is following a commonly recognized variant reading but his point holds good irrespective of whether it is 'and' or 'unto'.

Here then are two strands of truth: a redemption that is definite and yet good news and invitations that are to be addressed to all. So the question is, how do these two things, one particular and the other universal, stand related to each other? Can both be true? To that question we will return later, but more fundamental issues need to come first.

At Calvary We Learn of Forgiveness Consistent with Holiness and Justice

The entrance of sin into the human race created a problem with respect to the character of God in his dealings with men. Yet it is a problem about which we have no interest or comprehension until we come to be convicted that our sin deserves God's wrath and displeasure. Only when we are brought to see something of the enormity of sin do we discover why God's view of it is so different from our own. God loves righteousness with all the intensity of his being. And to love righteousness is necessarily to hate what is its opposite – in this his character is a pattern for us, 'Ye that love the Lord, hate evil' (*Psa.* 97:10). It is God's love of holiness which makes his judgment upon sin certain (*Psa.* 11:6–7). He 'will by no means clear the guilty' (*Exod.* 34:7). He 'will render to every man according to his works' (*Rom.* 2:6). Because he is holy and just he will never fail to act against the moral evil that is an affront to all that he is.[9]

---

[9] 'When God "swears in his wrath", that is, swears by that essential attribute of His nature which leads Him to hate and punish sin, no doubt can be entertained that this is a quality or property of God (*Psa.* 95:11). It is a perfection having its root in the moral excellence of God.' Smeaton, *Apostles' Doctrine of the Atonement,* p. 312.

Such is the problem created by sin. If God were to pardon sin without upholding his righteousness he would cease to be God; merely to waive the penalty that sin deserves would be to deny his perfection. How then can he be true to himself, how can he vindicate his holiness, how can he remain God, *and* at the same time forgive sin? How can he be righteous and not judge sin in righteousness? To put the same problem in another way, what can undo our past sin and remove its demerit in the sight of God? The whole world has no answer. It is a problem that no created intelligence can solve. An awakened conscience tells a man that even the omnipotence of God cannot undo the guilt of sin.

Only revelation can supply the answer and that answer can be stated in a single word: substitution – an exchange of places, a transference of responsibility – this is the good news to be proclaimed. The One has taken the place of the many, the sinless for the guilty: 'The LORD hath laid on him the iniquity of us all' (*Isa.* 53:6); 'The Lamb of God which takes away the sin of the world' (*John* 1:29); the Saviour who came 'not to be ministered unto but to minister and to give his life a ransom for many'(*Matt.* 20:28). God set forth Christ Jesus 'to be a propitiation' – a securing of divine favour – 'through faith in his blood' (*Rom.* 3:25). 'Through this man is preached unto you the forgiveness of sins, and by him all that believe are justified from all things from which ye could not be justified by the law of Moses' (*Acts* 13:38–39).

Here is a foremost truth disclosed at Calvary: God has upheld and vindicated his holiness! In the sufferings of Christ the divine justice which obstructed blessing coming

[10] John Owen, *Works*, vol. 9, (London: Banner of Truth, 1965) p. 594.

to those who deserve judgment has been satisfied. There is now favour and reconciliation for the very worst who has 'received the atonement' (*Rom.* 5:11). The pledge of God to pardon all who believe is bound up with the glory of his Son. In the cross God is both 'just and the justifier of him which believeth in Jesus' (*Rom.* 3:26), and there is no higher way for a sinner to glorify God than by trusting in Christ. In the words of John Owen, 'He was lifted up between heaven and earth, that all creatures might see that God had set him forth to be a propitiation.'[10] Accordingly the work of gospel preaching is to implore men on Christ's behalf to 'be reconciled to God' (*2 Cor.* 5:20). As Charles Hodge says, this does not mean, 'Reconcile yourselves to God', for the word is in the passive:

'Be reconciled,' that is, embrace the offer of reconciliation. The reconciliation is effected by the death of Christ. God is now propitious. He can be just and yet justify the ungodly. All we have to do is not to refuse the offered love of God.[11]

The last sentence brings us to another foremost truth.

[11] Charles Hodge, *Second Epistle to the Corinthians* (London: Banner of Truth, 1963), p. 147.

[12] *Suggestive Commentary on Romans,* vol. 1 (London: Dickinson, 1878), p. 239.

By Christ Crucified the Love of God and His Willingness to Save Is to Be Made Known to All People

To assert that the message of the cross is *wholly* one of divine love (as some have done) is to destroy its meaning. For it is only in the recognition of the holiness of God that the sufferings of Christ, which brought forth the cry, 'My God, My God, why have you forsaken me,' can be truly understood. Apart from divine justice that cry is inexplicable. In the words of Thomas Robinson, 'Sin is nowhere seen so terrible, nor the law so inflexible, as in the cross of Christ.'[12]

Yet if we ask why God was moved to exercise his holiness and justice in such a manner, at such a cost, in the sacrifice of his own beloved Son for our sins, the answer is 'God so loved the world'. And it was love that led Jesus first to undertake his sufferings, and then to invite all men to enter into the love which his death proclaims. It is the Puritan Thomas Watson who quotes the words of Augustine, 'The cross was a pulpit in which Christ preached his love to the world.'[13] On the same subject John Owen writes: 'There is no property of the nature of God which he doth so eminently design to glorify in the death of Christ as his love.'[14]

This brings us inevitably to John 3:16, 'God so loved the world . . .' On this text Smeaton says: 'These words of Christ plainly show that the biblical doctrine on this point is not duly

[13] Thomas Watson, *A Body of Divinity* (London: Banner of Truth, 1958), p. 175.
[14] Owen, *Works*, vol. 9, p. 604.

exhibited unless love receives a special prominence . . . If even justice were made paramount, the balance of truth would be destroyed.'[15]

But what is the love of God to which John 3:16 gives this prominence? Does it have reference to the elect only or to all men? Some have answered that its immediate purpose has to do with neither; because, they say, 'the world' here does not have numerical so much as ethical significance: it stands for 'the evil, the darkness, the sinner'.[16] God so loved those who are utterly contrary to himself that he gave his Son to die for them! As B. B. Warfield has written on the love of God in this text:

> It is not that it is so great that it is able to extend over the whole of a big world: it is so great that it is able to prevail over the Holy God's hatred and abhorrence of sin. For herein is love, that *God* could love the *world* – the world that lies in the evil one: that God who is all-holy and just and good, could so love this world that He gave His only begotten Son for it, – that He might not judge it, but that it might be saved.[17]

The same writer concludes: 'The whole debate as to whether the love here celebrated distributes itself to each and every man that enters into the composition of the world, or terminates on the elect alone chosen out of the world, lies thus outside the immediate scope of the passage.' But granting that the message of the cross is one of love to those who by nature are the enemies

[15] Smeaton, *Christ's Doctrine of the Atonement* (Edinburgh: Banner of Truth, 1991), pp. 45–46.

[16] See the usage of the word in John 7:7; 14:17, 22, 27, 30; 15:18–19; 16:8, 20, 33; 17:14.

[17] 'God's Immeasurable Love' in B. B. Warfield, *The Saviour of the World* (Edinburgh: Banner of Truth, 1991), p. 120.

of God, we are still faced with the fact that the text provides no justification for limiting this love to elect sinners. For if the elect are the 'world' that God loves, why is it that only some out of that world ('whosoever believes in him') come to salvation? There is surely a distinction in the text between the larger number who are the objects of love and the smaller number who believe. It would be a strange reading of John 3:16 to make those who believe correspond exclusively with 'the world' that God loves. Such a divine as John Calvin had no hesitation therefore in saying on John 3:16:

> Although there is nothing in the world deserving of God's favour, he nevertheless shows he is favourable to the whole lost world when he calls all without exception to faith in Christ, which is indeed an entry into life.[18]

If this is so, it is proof enough that there is a general proclamation of the love of God which comes to men in the preaching of the cross. Individuals everywhere may be directed, as Nicodemus was directed, to God's love for the unworthy. We are by no means dependent on John 3:16 alone for this understanding. Surely the same truth shines throughout our Lord's ministry. He, 'the Friend of sinners', did not limit love to the disciples, nor yet to those whom he knew would become disciples. We read, 'When he saw the multitudes, he was moved with compassion for them'(*Matt.* 9:36). Moreover we find this tender compassion individualized: of the rich young ruler, who turned away from Christ in unbelief, we are explicitly told, 'Jesus, looking at him,

---

[18] Calvin, *The Gospel According to John, 1-10*, trans., T. H. L. Parker (Grand Rapids: Eerdmans, 1979), p. 74.

loved him' (*Mark* 10:21). What but that same love can explain such words as, 'You will not come unto me that you might have life' (*John* 5:40)? Or the tears that accompanied, 'O Jerusalem, Jerusalem, thou that killest the prophets, and stonest them which are sent unto thee, how often would I have gathered thy children together, even as a hen gathereth her chickens under her wings, and ye would not!'(*Luke* 13:34; *Matt* 23:37)? 'Love towards *all mankind in general,*' John Owen wrote, is enforced upon us by the example of Christ's 'own love and goodness, which are extended unto all'.[19] And Owen encouraged his hearers to dwell on the 'love of Christ, in his invitations of sinners to come unto him that they may be saved'.[20]

Elsewhere the same writer says: 'There is nothing that at the last day will tend more immediately to the advancement of the glory of God, in the inexcusableness of them who obey not the gospel, than this, that terms of peace, in the blessed way of forgiveness, were freely tendered unto them.'[21]

Some have sought to escape from the force of Christ's example by referring it to his human nature and not to his divine. But as R. L. Dabney comments: 'It would impress the common Christian mind with a most painful feeling to be thus seemingly taught that holy humanity is more generous and tender than God.'[22]

Christ's example, that reveals the very character of God, remains the permanent standard for the church. The same love of which he spoke to Nicodemus, and which he showed to

---

[19] Owen, *Works*, vol. 15, p. 70. The italics are in Owen. [20] *Works*, vol. 1, p. 422.

[21] Owen, *Works*, vol. 6, p. 530.

[22] R. L. Dabney, *Discussions: Evangelical and Theological,* vol. 1 (London: Banner of Truth, 1967), p. 308. 'It is our happiness to believe that when we see Jesus weeping over lost Jerusalem, we have "seen the Father", we have received an insight into he divine benevolence and pity.' An evidence of this can be seen in the pleading of God with sin-

the multitude, lies in his command that 'repentance unto remission of sins should be preached in his name among all nations, beginning at Jerusalem' (*Luke* 24:47). And the apostles understood it when they preached indiscriminately to the Jerusalem sinners, who had rejected the Son of God, the astonishing news that God has sent Jesus 'to bless you, in turning away every one of you from his iniquities' (*Acts* 3:26).[23]

Universal gospel preaching is proof of the reality of universal divine love. It is the same love of which we read in Ezekiel 33:11: 'As I live, saith the Lord God, I have no pleasure in the death of the wicked; but that the wicked turn from his way and live: turn ye from your evil ways; for why will ye die?' When the Pharisees complained of Christ, 'This man receives sinners, and eats with them,' Jesus responded by speaking of the character of God: he is like the father of the prodigal son who 'saw him and had compassion, and ran and fell on his neck and kissed him' (*Luke* 15:20)[24] Christ's unwillingness that men should be lost is the same as the Father's. He

---

ners in the Old Testament, e.g., 'For thus saith the Lord GOD, the Holy One of Israel; In returning and rest shall ye be saved; in quietness and confidence shall be your strength: and ye would not' (*Isa.* 30:15). 'Our utmost that we can, by zeal for his glory or compassion unto your souls,' writes Owen on proclaiming the invitations of the gospel, 'comes infinitely short of his own pressing earnestness herein.' Owen, *Works*, vol. 6, p. 517.

[23] For the way in which the gospel message is individualized in apostolic testimony see also Acts 2:38; 3:19; Colossians 1: 28; 1 Timothy 2:4; 2 Peter 3:9.

[24] ' It would hardly be in accord with our Lord's intention to press the point that the prodigal was destined to come to repentance, and that, therefore, the father's attitude towards him portrays the attitude of God toward the elect only, and not toward every sinner as such.' Geerhardus Vos, 'The Scriptural Doctrine of the Love of God,' in *Redemptive History and Biblical Interpretation,* ed. R. B. Gaffin (Phillipsburg, NJ: Presbyterian and Reformed, 1980), p. 443.

desires that all men everywhere should turn and live. As John Murray has written:

> There is a love of God which goes forth to lost men and is manifested in the manifold blessings which all men without distinction enjoy, a love in which non-elect persons are embraced, and a love which comes to its highest expression in the entreaties, overtures and demands of gospel proclamation.[25]

We conclude that the death of Christ is to be preached to all, and preached in the conviction that there is love for all. 'In the gospel,' said an eminent preacher of the Scottish Highlands, 'the provision of God's love for the salvation of sinners is revealed and offered . . . Faith is a believing God as speaking to me – a receiving of what is said as true, because it is the testimony of God, and receiving it as true in its bearing on my own case as a sinner because it is addressed by God to me.'[26] Another Scots Calvinistic leader put it still more strongly in the words: 'Men evangelized cannot go to hell but over the bowels of God's great mercies. They must wade to it through the blood of Christ.'[27]

[25] Murray, *Collected Writings,* vol. 1, p. 68.
[26] MS sermon of Dr John Kennedy of Dingwall on Mark 16:16, preached on 10 January 1864.
[27] John Duncan, quoted in *'Just a Talker': The Sayings of Dr John Duncan,* (Edinburgh: Banner of Truth, 1997) p. 221.

PARTICULAR AND GENERAL LOVE

'Particular' and 'general' are not words that have explicit biblical warrant. The love of God is not presented to us in Scripture in categories at once distinguishable from each other. As Donald Carson writes:

> We must not view these ways of talking about the love of God as independent, compartmentalized, *loves* of God . . . as if each were hermetically sealed off from the other . . . If you absolutize any one of these ways in which the Bible speaks of the love of God, you will generate a false system that squeezes out other important things the Bible says, thus finally distorting your vision of God.[28]

This admission is important. Language cannot reach the immensity of the reality; and yet the terms general and particular, or common and special, represent a distinction that can be justified, as it has in fact been by many teachers of the church. John Calvin preached it. He does not hesitate to speak of 'the first degree of love' in redemption, and this, he says, 'extends to all men, inasmuch as Christ Jesus reaches out his arms to call and allure all men both great and small, and to win them to

[28] D. A. Carson, *The Difficult Doctrine of the Love of God* (Wheaton: Crossway, 2000), pp. 23, 75.

[29] John Calvin, *Sermons on Deuteronomy* (Edinburgh: Banner of Truth, 1987), p. 167. 'The second degree of love' is 'a special love unto those to whom the gospel is preached . . . the third love that God shows us: which is, that he not only causes the gospel to be preached unto us, but also makes us to feel the power thereof, so we know him to be our father and saviour.'

him.' This love he goes on to distinguish from 'special love'.[29] 'As he regards men with paternal love, so also he would have them to be saved.'[30] Puritans had no problem in speaking of 'God's unspeakable love to mankind', or in asserting that 'God hath a general love to all the creatures'.[31] Other Calvinistic preachers down to C. H. Spurgeon all made a similar distinction.[32] More recently Geerhardus Vos wrote:

> We certainly have a right to say that the love which God originally bears toward man as created in His image survives in the form of compassion under the reign of sin. This being so, when the sinner comes in contact with the gospel of grace, it is natural for God to desire that he should accept its offer and be saved.[33]

[30] Calvin, *Commentaries on Jeremiah*, vol. 5 (Edinburgh: Banner of Truth, 1989), p. 423 (on *Lam.* 3:33).

[31] See, for instance, Thomas Manton on John 3:16 in *Works*, vol. 2 (Edinburgh, Banner of Truth, 1993), p. 340; Hugh Binning, *Christian Love* (Edinburgh: Banner of Truth, 2004), p. 6.

[32] Further on Spurgeon and this whole issue, see my *Spurgeon v. Hyper-Calvinism* (Edinburgh: Banner of Truth, 1995).

[33] Vos, *Redemptive History*, p. 443–4. Vos adds: 'But this universal love should be always so conceived as to leave room for the fact that God, for sovereign reasons, has not chosen to bestow upon its objects that higher love which not merely desires, but purposes and works out the salvation of some.' This truth gives rise to the objection, How can God be said to desire what he does not effectively will to be accomplished? The only answer is that he does so desire, and that in the sovereignty of his grace, he has not chosen to will the salvation of all men in the same manner. As John Howe says on Christ's tears over Jerusalem: 'It is unavoidably imposed upon us to believe that God is truly unwilling for some things, which he doth not think fit to interpose his omnipotency to hinder; and is truly willing of some things which he doth not put forth his omnipotency to effect.' 'The Redeemer's Tears Wept over Lost Souls', *Works of John Howe*, vol. 2 (London: Tegg, 1848), p. 359. A helpful exegetical study by John Piper, 'Are There Two Wills in God? Divine Election and God's Desire for All to Be Saved,' will be found in T. R. Schreiner and B. A. Ware, eds., *The Grace of God and the Bondage of the Will*, vol. 1 (Grand Rapids: Baker, 1995), pp. 107–131.

If a distinction between general and special love is correct, does it provide a solution to the problem of how the sufferings of Christ can be said to be both particular and universal? No, this is not a solution, for it provides no answer to the question as to how Christ can be sincerely offered to those whom he did not represent in his sufferings.

To provide an answer to that question some have argued that, if the invitations of the gospel are universal, then the atonement itself must also be universal. Propitiation must have been made for the sins of all men. Others have taken the opposite course. Believing that the atonement is definite and particular they proceed to deny any universal offer of salvation. They say Christ only meant the gospel invitation to be universal in order that by its proclamation the elect among all men may be gathered in. There is, according to this belief, no message of love for all.[34]

These alternatives have their attraction in rendering consistent what we do not otherwise understand, but with the evidence of Scripture before us they cannot be right. The reality is that we are faced with truths that far outreach our understanding. Making that point on this subject, Calvin wrote on the words of Ezekiel 18:23: 'It is not surprising that our eyes should be blinded by intense light, so that we cannot

[34] This kind of objection has long been heard. Thomas Chalmers regretted the teaching of 'those Particular Redemptionists who explain away the universality of the gospel, by telling us that it only bears on some men in all nations.' *Sabbath Scripture Readings*, vol. 1 (Edinburgh: Sutherland and Knox, 1848), p. 173. For a powerful sermon by the same author on 'The Universality of the Gospel Offer,' see *Works of Thomas Chalmers*, vol. 10 (Glasgow: Collins, n.d.[1835?]). Chalmers was at the centre of the evangelical revival in Scotland in the early nineteenth century, yet he also believed in particular redemption and insisted against Thomas Erskine, 'All men are not pardoned – but all men have the pardon laid down for their acceptance.' See *Letters of Thomas Chalmers*, pp. 348–9.

certainly judge how God wishes all to be saved, and yet has devoted all the reprobate to eternal destruction.'[35] And on how God can be said to love in different ways Calvin says:

> True it is, that to speak properly, God has no divers affections: we must not imagine so: but I handle these matters according to our capacity, and we must consider of God's love according to our slenderness, because we cannot attain to his high majesty as is said afore, and therefore even he himself also uttereth himself to us according to our ability.[36]

Similarly, Thomas Crawford has said that the subject, 'far exceeds the power and compass of our faculties . . . it may be that the missing link that is needful, may be hidden from our view in that profound abyss of God's everlasting counsels which we cannot fathom.'[37]

Rowland Hill, the English evangelist at the end of the eighteenth century, was once present at 'a diet of catechizing' in Scotland. After he had also put some questions which were correctly answered, a grey-haired man asked if he might put a question to Mr Hill: 'Sir,' he said, 'can you reconcile the universal call o' the gospel wi' the doctrine o' a particler eleck?' Hill was right to reply promptly that he could not.

---

[35] *Commentaries on Ezekiel*, vol. 2 (Edinburgh: Calvin Translation Soc., 1850), p. 247.

[36] Calvin, *Deuteronomy*, p. 167.

[37] Thomas J. Crawford, *The Doctrine of Holy Scripture Respecting the Atonement* (Edinburgh: Blackwood, 1888), p. 510. Smeaton speaks similarly: ' A special atonement and invitations sincerely made on the ground of it to mankind indefinitely are quite compatible. They will be found to meet at some point though their junction be beyond our present line of vision.' *Christ's Doctrine of the Atonement*, p. 380.

While the distinction between the general and the special or particular love of God does not, therefore, give us all the light we might ask for, it is nonetheless of much importance. It is necessary for believers to understand the special nature of God's love to them. 'The Son of God loved me and gave himself for me' (*Gal.* 2:20), is not a statement that gives security to all. To deny the special love of God, and to believe that Christ loves all men equally, is to suppose that Christ has done no more for those the Father has given to him than for mankind at large. But if Christians are no more loved than those who will finally be lost, the decisive factor in salvation becomes, not God's grace and love, but something in them, and their perseverance becomes dependent upon themselves.[38] To widen the atonement, and to speak of it only in terms of general love, is to take away its *saving* power. The believer in Christ needs to know that the love which embraces him is eternal, almighty, and immutable. It does not hang upon his faith for it went before faith.

However, if one facet of truth is needed by the believer, another is important for the unconverted. If there is no love except special love for the elect, then no one has any right to apprehend any love in God for them *before* they have evidence of their election, which is to say, before they are converted. And that would mean that preachers must not speak of the love of Christ indefinitely to all their unconverted hearers. Such an omission has to subvert gospel preaching. It would no longer be 'good news' for all – no longer an appeal 'not to refuse the offered love of God' – it would be a system closed to all except those who find some reason for faith other than the plain invitations of Christ.

---

[38] It was not an accident that Methodism departed from Protestant evangelicalism in rejecting the final perseverance of saints.

The nature of conversion is an issue involved here. Are men brought into the kingdom of God by an action of God that bypasses the mind and will, or are those faculties involved in the great change? Does Christ draw men to himself irrespective of their thoughts and their consent? The scriptural answer has to be that conversion *includes* hearing and understanding; the Holy Spirit uses truth to convince of sin; that is the first work.

But conviction of sin is not enough to bring men to Christ. Conviction of sin only speaks of God's holiness, it tells the sinner nothing of God's willingness to pardon; it does nothing to remove the suspicion - common to fallen man – that God is against him and unconcerned for his happiness. For that further truth is needed. It is only the disclosure of love which can persuade the sinner of God's readiness and willingness to pardon, and thus the necessity that love be made known to all indefinitely in the free offer of the gospel. Love is the great attraction. Love stands foremost in the gospel appeal. 'It is not the over-heavy load of sin,' says John Bunyan, 'but the discovery of mercy . . . that makes a man come to Jesus Christ . . . Behold how the promises, invitations, calls, and encouragements, like lilies, lie round about thee! Take heed that thou dost not tread them under foot, sinner. With promises, did I say? Yea, he hath mixed all those with his own name, his Son's name; also, with the names of mercy, goodness, compassion, love, pity, grace, forgiveness, pardon, and what not, that he might encourage the coming sinner.' [39]

[39] Bunyan, *Works*, vol. 1 (Edinburgh: Banner of Truth, 1991), pp. 286, 298. 'Men must see something in Jesus Christ, else they will not come to him.' (p. 295). A fine example of preaching that pleads with men can be seen in the closing pages of Bunyan's *Come and Welcome to Jesus Christ* (Edinburgh: Banner of Truth, 2004), from which these quotations are taken.

On the same point, John Owen wrote:

Christ draws none to himself whether they will or no; but he casts on their minds, hearts, and wills the cords of his grace and love, working in them powerfully, working on them kindly, to cause them to choose him . . . Drawing grace is manifested in, and drawing love proceeds from, the sufferings of Christ on the cross.[40]

This love is to be proclaimed as 'good news' not to men as elect but to men as sinners.[41] That is why any message that would not include love to individuals until there is evidence of their election turns the gospel upside down. It withholds the very truth most conducive to bringing souls to rest in Christ. Without question, history teaches us that the evangelists most used of God have all been men for whom love has been the main theme.[42] Our sin must be discovered, says Richard Sibbes, 'to drive us out of ourselves,' but then, 'there must be a great deal of persuasion to still the accusing conscience of a sinner, to set it down, make it quiet, and persuade it of God's love'.[43]

---

[40] *Works*, vol. 9, p. 592.

[41] Ibid., vol. 6, p. 523. Owen is including both the universal and the particular when he says that the freeness of God's mercy does not interfere with the efficacy. 'Though he [God] proclaim pardon in the blood of Christ indefinitely, according to the fullness and excellency of it, yet he giveth out his quickening grace to enable men to receive it as he pleaseth; for he hath mercy on whom he will have mercy. But this lies in the thing itself; the way is opened and prepared, and it is not because men cannot enter, but because they will not, that they do not enter.' p. 529.

[42] Evidence for this statement is vast; I give some of it in my book, *Pentecost —Today?* (Edinburgh: Banner of Truth, 1998), p. 90–9.

[43] Sibbes, *Works*, vol. 2, (Edinburgh: Banner of Truth, 1983) p. 186.

Persuading men of God's love is the great calling of the Christian ministry. It is part of preaching 'to root out all the secret reserves of unbelief concerning God's unwillingness to give mercy, grace and pardon to sinners'.[44] It cannot be done without conviction in the preacher that this love is a wonderful reality, and that it is to be pressed on all his hearers.

Yet, it may be asked, if this love is not necessarily saving, should the distinction between 'general' and 'special' not be made clear to people when the gospel is being presented? The answer has to be no, for Scripture itself makes no such distinction in the presentation of the gospel to the lost. And the reason why it does not do so is plain: it is not a doctrine either of special love or of general love that is to be offered to sinners; it is rather *Christ himself.* More than that, it is not ultimately preachers who offer Christ to others; but Christ – divine love incarnate – who speaks in the gospel and offers himself fully and freely to the most undeserving, if they will but receive him. 'Christ offers himself in mercy to the worst soul,'[45] even, as Whitefield used to say, to 'the devil's castaways'.

The relation of the preacher's role to Christ's is well stated by Robert Candlish:

I go to the crowd of criminals, shut up in prison, under sentence of death; and my message is, not that in consequence of Christ's death I have now to offer them all liberty to go out free; – but that Christ himself is there, even at the door; in whom, if they apply to him, they will find One who

[44] Owen, *Works*, vol. 6, p. 504.
[45] Sibbes, *Works,* vol. 2, p. 187. 'It is our office, thus to lay open and offer the riches of Christ.'

can meet every accusation against them, and enrich them with every blessing. I refer them and point them to himself – to himself alone . . . I do not speak to them of a certain amount of atoning virtue purchased by the obedience and death of Christ, as if it were a store laid up for general use, from which they may take what they need. I speak to them of Christ as being himself the atonement, and summon them to a personal dealing with him accordingly . . . a present Saviour now, as well as then, having in his hand a special pardon and special grace for every one who will resort to him – and nothing for any who will not.[46]

Candlish's point is of vital importance. Not only does evangelism not depend on the existence of a universal atonement, any making of saving faith to rest on a statement that 'Christ has died for you' is dangerously wrong. As Spurgeon, one of the foremost evangelists in English church history, said:

You may believe that Jesus Christ died for you, and may believe what is not true; you may believe that which will bring you no sort of good whatever. That is not saving faith. The man that has saving faith afterwards attains to the conviction that Christ died for him, but it is not of the essence of saving faith. Do not get that into your head, or it will ruin you. Do not say, 'I believe that Jesus Christ died for me,' and because of that feel that you are saved. I pray you to remember that the genuine faith that saves has for its main element – trust

[46] Robert S. Candlish, *The Atonement: Its Reality, Completeness, and Extent* (Edinburgh: Nelson, 1861), pp. 232–233.

– absolute rest of the whole soul – on the Lord Jesus Christ to save me, whether he died in particular or in special to save me or not, and relying, as I am, wholly and alone on him, I am saved. Afterwards I come to perceive that I have a special interest in the Saviour's blood.[47]

CONCLUSIONS

1. *This whole discussion shows how truth needs to be taught in its biblical proportions, and with consideration of the condition and circumstances of the hearers.*

Not all truths are equally important for all and on all occasions. The so-called Five Points of Calvinism are important to distinguish certain truths from opposing tenets, but they are not all equally important for the presentation of the gospel to the lost. Whitefield was right to admire the words of John Bradford, 'Let a man go to the school of faith and repentance, before he goes to the university of election and predestination.'[48] The preaching of Christ crucified to the unconverted requires the presentation of his Person, the cost of his substitution for sinners, and the immensity of the divine love for sinners; it does not require explanations of the extent of the atonement. To quote Candlish again: 'It is irrelevant here

[47] *Metropolitan Tabernacle Pulpit,* vol. 58, pp. 583–4.
[48] *George Whitefield's Journals* (London: Banner of Truth, 1960), p. 491.
[49] Candlish, *The Atonement,* p. 202.

to raise any question as to the extent, or even as to the sufficiency of the atonement. It is enough that it is sufficient for all who will avail themselves of it.'[49]

In this connection it is noteworthy that in the preaching of one of the most effective Calvinistic evangelists of the twentieth century, D. Martyn Lloyd-Jones, it was generally impossible to tell from his gospel preaching that he held to a particular and definite atonement.

2. *It is not the preacher's business to explain the unexplainable.*

Where the Scripture sees no contradictions in its state-ments it is not our responsibility to answer objections that may be raised. For instance, 'How is it consistent with the unity of God's nature to speak of his possessing both general and particular love? How can the truth of his anger towards the wicked be compatible with the existence of any common love? Can compassion and wrath coexist in God's attitude towards sinners?'

Much error has come about through attempts to offer explanations of such questions. It ought to be enough, as I have said, to stand by what Scripture asserts. We are to be humble before the conviction that God's thoughts are far above our own. Truths that look contradictory to us are not so in the light of heaven. We are told, for instance, that God's wrath is revealed against the same men who are *also* the object of goodness and longsuffering that would lead them to repentance (*Rom.* 1:18; 2:4). For Israel's rejection of the Saviour 'the wrath [was] come upon them to the uttermost'; yet God's compassionate entreaties towards them continued:

'To Israel he says, All day long I have stretched forth my hands unto a disobedient and gainsaying people' (*1 Thess.* 2:16; *Rom.* 10:21). It is of men under God's wrath that Scripture says he is 'not willing that any should perish, but that all should come to repentance' (*2 Pet.* 3:9).

These are truths to be preached without hesitation and without distracting needy souls with questions of controversy.

3. *Discussion of the doctrines of grace becomes dangerous when interest in them is more theoretical than practical.*

Truth is given to men in order to their salvation (*2 Tim.* 3:15). If the presentation of the gospel ceases to be the first concern we have already gone wrong. To possess a knowledge of profound truths without *seeing* them at work in the salvation of sinners is not what Scripture commends. All knowledge that does not lead to practical love is to be pitied.

In this connection, words once spoken by William Roberts in a gathering of Calvinistic Methodist preachers in Wales, are worthy of repetition. Aspects of Calvinistic truth were under discussion, and the meeting was proceeding in such a way that Roberts believed their unity was being needlessly threatened. After a younger man had referred to the difficulty he found in preaching on election, Roberts rose to speak. He said he was glad to see that the young man evidently believed that 'there is a greater purpose to preaching than mere talking', and questioned whether they would ever be 'sufficient preachers' to preach election. 'I do not know who of us – if any – is such.' Then he went on:

But should you ever attempt it, strive to view it yourself, and to so present it to your listeners, in the relationships in which you find it in God's Book. Particularly, do not keep it afar off in eternity; it will do no good to anyone there. Bring it down to the chapel, down to the midst of the people. There it will save. It is in its operation that we will understand election, if we will ever understand it.

Consider a large, complex machine, with its various wheels, pipes, hooks and chains, all interweaving and interlocking with one another. It is the engineer who understands its design and can explain it, in and of itself, its various parts, and the relationships of each part with the others so as to make one engine. But I can see it in operation. And an ordinary, illiterate man, knowing nothing of the laws of Mechanics and ignorant of the names which the engineer has for the various parts of the machine, he can make use of it and work with it, to achieve the end that was in view when it was designed and built. And it would be ludicrous to see those ignorant workers proceeding to argue amongst themselves as to the composition of the machine, rather than using it to purpose.

When you preach election, preach of it at work. Beware of speculating boldly and investigating in detail into the workings of the internal parts of the machine, and avoid bringing your listeners into the same temptation. Show the worth and glory of the machine by demonstrating it at work. Show the worth of the election of grace by depicting it as saving those who cannot save themselves. That is the view of it given in the Bible, and that, as far as I know, is the only worth it holds for the sinner. If this were not so I do not think the Gospel would acknowledge any relationship to it. But, on the contrary, upon understanding election properly, we find that it not only belongs to the Gospel but that it is one of the sweetest parts of it . . . it is life itself for such a dull, helpless, stubborn creature as myself that God has a provision, in his infinite grace, that meets my condition, and that he will never see in me anything that could turn out a disappointment to him, for he knew my whole history long before I knew anything of it myself.[50]

Calvinistic belief surely loses its attractiveness when the wisdom of this illustration is forgotten.

4. If controversy among Christians on the atonement is sometimes unavoidable, let it be conducted in the most guarded language.

It is to be deeply regretted that this subject has too often led to God-dishonouring debate among Christians. Much time has been lost in argument and in the promotion of different views. But concern for purity in the faith can never justify believers in making the cross a subject of strife among themselves. We are shocked when we read that at Calvary there were soldiers gambling – 'casting lots' – over who should possess the Saviour's clothing. But our conduct is not so very different if we fall to wrangling about our crucified Saviour. In his day, when there were such disputes over the doctrine of the atonement, John Elias found it necessary to say:

[50] *The Atonement Controversy in Welsh Theological Literature and Debate, 1707–1841,* Owen Thomas, translated by John Aaron (1874; first English translation, Edinburgh: Banner of Truth, 2002), pp. 343–4. This book gives a sad demonstration of how unprofitable controversy may be.

The conversation of many respecting the death of Christ is often very unbecoming. It is that of persons that have no corresponding feeling, no brokenness of heart and humility. They converse about it in a dry, carnal, and presumptuous manner. They never talk about it as the only way a person ever saw to save his life, when pursued by the holy law, and condemned by the justice of God.[51]

5. No subject places higher demands upon the gospel preacher than this one.

If the cross is the pulpit from which the love of God is to be made known, why is it not more widely heard among us? Has our emphasis moved from the apostolic centre? Sometimes a lack of concentration on the love of God is justified by the argument that love is too prominent in the false religion of our times. It is true that all speaking of 'the love of God' apart from Christ is a false gospel, but the prevalence of the false ought to make us the more ready to preach the true. The confidence which non-Christians sometimes say they have in divine love is not in the love of God at all.

The source of our weakness as evangelists is that we are not living close enough to the fountainhead of love. Faithfulness and conscientiousness may be enough to enable us to say something on the law and judgments of God, but we cannot speak well of the love of God to sinners unless we are

[51] *John Elias, Life, Letters and Essays*, p. 362. The volume mentioned above, *The Atonement Controversy*, is replete with evidence that his words were not unnecessary.

personally familiar with it and persuaded of it. What is at the forefront of our experience is going to be at the forefront of our preaching. It is 'divine love', writes Edwards, by which 'a minister of the gospel is a *burning light* . . . with ardent love to the souls of men, and desires for their salvation'.[52] 'Let him speak of love,' says Bunyan, 'that is *taken* with love, that is *captivated* with love, that is *carried away* with love . . . These are the men that *sweeten* churches and bring glory to God.'[53]

Of all the graces needed to make Christ known the greatest is love. The preachers who have had much of this grace, even though sometimes deficient in other respects, have been those owned of God to a remarkable degree. This is the reason why the Wesleyan Methodists were once so greatly used to deprive Satan of many of his subjects. They were right to sing:

> The arms of love that compass me
> Would all mankind embrace.

Love explains why men have been able to live with a passion for the conversion of others. 'He loved the world that hated him,' wrote Cowper of Whitefield, 'the tear that fell upon his Bible was sincere.' 'I could bear to be torn in pieces,' said Henry Martyn, 'if I could but see eyes of faith directed to the Redeemer.'

Where is this love to be found but in the Saviour himself? Our prayer must be to be 'delivered from all coldness to Christ's death and passion,' and God answers that prayer by giving us a new, felt, understanding of texts we may long have known. The

---

[52] Jonathan Edwards, *Works*, vol. 2, p. 957.
[53] Ibid., pp. 39, 35.

Scriptures can be illuminated afresh to us as they were once to an Australian Methodist, William Reeves. Before going to his trade as usual on the morning of 16 August, 1846, the following occurred as he read John 3 in family worship:

> When I came to the exceeding precious lines, the 16th and 17th verses, the Lord in a most extraordinary manner broke in on my soul by the light of his Holy Spirit. He filled my whole soul with pure light, with fullness of joy, and holy love: all language fails to express what I felt. I saw and felt as I never saw before, that the Almighty did not love me in word only, but in deed and truth, in bestowing that unspeakable gift of his well-beloved Son: and I saw so clearly the precious love of his dear Son so sweetly blending with the Father's, that they became together one mighty ocean of unfathomable love.[54]

The cross remains the pulpit of God's love!

[54] *Usefulness* (Edinburgh: Nelson, 1871), p. 80.

Additional Notes

John Calvin, 1509–64: Gospel Preaching

Isaiah had preached on the death and resurrection of our Lord Jesus Christ: as if he had displayed the banner to declare that everyone should come to be reconciled to God, and that poor sinners should be received to mercy, that their satisfaction and righteousness is altogether ready, and that God desireth nothing but to be merciful to those who seek him.[55]

Thomas Chalmers, 1780–1847: God is Love

There is a moral, a depth and intensity of meaning, a richness of sentiment that the Bible calls unsearchable, in the cross of Christ. It tells a sinful world that God is righteousness; and it as clearly and emphatically tells us that God is love.

[55] Calvin, *Thirteen Sermons,* p. 61.

But for the purpose of making this doctrine available to ourselves personally, we must view the love of God, not as a vague and inapplicable generality, but as specially directed, nay actually proffered, and that pointedly and individually to each of us. It is not sufficiently adverted to by inquirers, nor sufficiently urged by ministers, that the constitution of the gospel warrants this appropriation of its blessings by each man for himself . . . It is a message of good news to all people . . . The blessings of the gospel are as accessible to all who will, as are the water or the air or any of the cheap and common bounties of nature. The element of Heaven's love is in as universal diffusion among the dwelling-places of men, as is the atmosphere they breathe in. It solicits admittance at every door; and the ignorance or unbelief of man are the only obstacles which it has to struggle with. It is commensurate with the species; and may be tendered, urgently and honestly tendered, to each individual of the human family.[56]

WILLIAM NEVINS, 1797–1835: THE EXTENT OF THE ATONEMENT

In regard to the extent of the atonement, I would just say that it is so extensive that none will ever be lost by reason of any deficiency in it. It is extensive as it need be; so extensive, that on the ground of it, salvation is sincerely and freely offered to all; so extensive, that if all should accept the offer, all would be saved. Is not this extensive enough? It is limited only in this sense, that it was made with a special reference to those who will ultimately

[56] *Works of Thomas Chalmers*, vol. 10, pp. 188–91.

be saved by it. The foundation is broad enough to receive every soul – all the souls of all men. And all the sins of all these souls, though they be very many and very great, Christ's blood has still efficacy to cleanse away. Therefore, let each one come to Christ, and secure himself an interest in the atonement. Let this be the first anxiety – the first work. Does anything equal it in point of importance?[57]

John Bonar, 1799–1863: The Universal Offer and the Compassion of God

Two things are evidently required, in order that these calls may be warrantably addressed to all, and all may have full warrant to comply with them. 1st, That there should be a Saviour provided – and 2nd, That that Saviour being provided, his salvation should be freely offered to us. Christ is an all-sufficient Saviour – having all that sinners need. Christ as thus all-sufficient is freely offered to all, – and this offer is conveyed to us, upon the testimony of God, and comes to each as "the word of salvation" sent to himself.

The call to come is thus itself the assurance of welcome. As it would be presumption to come without an invitation, so it is presumption to hesitate when that invitation is sent . . . Yes, Christ is God's gift to mankind sinners. The cross is God's ordinance for the salvation of men, and Christ is dead for you to come to – for you to live by. God calleth you by ten thousand expostulations and entreaties which he sends in his Word. Christ calleth you by his

---

[57] *Select Remains of the Rev. William Nevins* (New York: Taylor, 1836).

sufferings – by his death – by his tears of compassion – and by his entreaties of grace. The Holy Spirit calleth you by every one of those words of mercy and of warning, and by every conviction and impression which they awaken in the heart. Thy God hath found thee out, not with words of condemnation, but with words of mercy. His words are all as fresh and full of love as if first now, and first by you, they have been heard in human language. With these words of gracious compassion doth he once more overtake you – beseeching you to turn and live - assuring you that in no wise you shall be cast out. O sons of men, his words mean all that they say, and infinitely more than human words can say; they are drops of the compassion of God . . . God directly, personally, and earnestly beseeches us to be reconciled to him - eternal life in offer, Christ in offer, everlasting blessedness in offer, and every one either receiving or rejecting these offers. Rest not until the voice of Christ to the sons of men be answered by you in the first breathings of the Spirit of adoption, "I will arise and go to my Father." [58]

[58] 'The Universal Calls and Invitations of the Gospel Consistent with the Total Depravity of Man, and Particular Redemption', sermon on Proverbs 8:4, 6, in *The Free Church Pulpit* (Perth: Dewar, 1844).

A SCOTTISH CHRISTIAN HERITAGE

ISBN 0 85151 930 X
416 pp., clothbound

'What a heritage! Here are some of the giants – John Knox, Robert Bruce, Thomas Chalmers, Horatius Bonar, among others – who grace the history of Scotland . . . A thrilling story of those who lived and died for the Gospel. The last chapter is the saddest, since it charts the capitulation of the Scottish Church to the assaults of criticism, which led to a loss of belief in the divine inspiration of Scripture. It all happened virtually within a generation. Iain Murray has been a prolific author and this book, like his others, is well-written, reads well, and focuses on issues which are still relevant today.

CLC World

Once more we are in debt to Iain Murray for a superb historical survey. He does not set out to write a comprehensive church history of Scotland, but takes his readers through four centuries, providing selective biographies and addressing certain issues. Most chapters end with 'lessons' or 'observations'. This is another lavish Banner production: a book to last, a book to keep and then bequeath to a rising generation that needs to know its Christian heritage . . . A must-read.

New Life

All in all, this is an excellent volume. The author's knowledge of, and love for, his theme is everywhere apparent.

British Church Newspaper

EVANGELICALISM DIVIDED:
A RECORD OF CRUCIAL CHANGE
IN THE YEARS 1950 – 2000

ISBN 0 85151 783 8
352 pp., clothbound

'The book is a page turner from first to last . . . It left me asking, "Has the last fifty years seen evangelicals broaden the road to the extent that the Christian message is compromised and uncertain?" '

Peter Breckwoldt, *Church of England Newspaper*

'Murray's critique is as kind as it is revealing and devastating. The icons of modern evangelism are shown as falling into egregious strategic errors which have weakened the evangelical faith at its very core. The bridges built to reach the mainstream became a two-way street by which those who sought to influence the liberals were themselves influenced.'

R. C. Sproul, *Table Talk*

'Murray presents a convincing argument with cogent evidence. His ability to concentrate on the bigger picture, without ignoring necessary details, ensures that he takes the reader with him. There is no doubt that there will be readers of this book who will take exception to some of his conclusions, but the broad thesis stands firm. This book is probably one of the most important church history books published in 2000 and every church leader ought to read it.'

Brian Talbot, *Scottish Baptist Website*

JONATHAN EDWARDS:
A NEW BIOGRAPHY

ISBN 0 85151 704 8
536 pp., paperback, illustrated

'This is my book of the year, for which I have waited a life-time.'

Graham Miller, *Australian Presbyterian Life*

'Surely Murray's fine biography will gain the audience it deserves.'

William and Mary Quarterly

'A biography giving proper weight to the spiritual life and stature of Jonathan Edwards was needed . . . This is what Iain Murray has provided and he has done the job well. He has unique skill in this area.'

J. I. Packer

'Murray provides a standard of excellence among Christian biographers. Edwards' life, especially as he presents it, offers significant challenge to Christians. No one should come away from it without being challenged to a deeper commitment to Jesus Christ, a greater desire for prayer and wholeheartedness, and a stronger resolve to be a doer of the Word as well as a hearer.'

Moody Monthly

REVIVAL AND REVIVALISM:
THE MAKING AND MARRING OF AMERICAN EVANGELICALISM, 1750-1858

ISBN 0 85151 660 2
480 pp., cloth-bound, illustrated

'It is a rare book that hits both head and heart in a way that turns a life. Revival and Revivalism had that effect on me, providing a clear and convincing perspective on the role and importance of revivals in American church history, bringing me to a new stage in my spiritual pilgrimage, and giving me a new hope for the prospects of the gospel in the world.'

Scott McCullough, *Blue Banner* (Pittsburgh)

'Murray has uncovered much fresh information which, I suspect, will surprise and delight even the most seasoned reader . . . a valuable new resource.'

Garth M. Rosell, *American Presbyterians*

'Murray's main point is also theologically compelling: when religion becomes something that humans work up for God (i.e. "revivalism") instead of something God graciously bestows upon repentant sinners (i.e. "revival"), the integrity of the faith is at stake .'

Mark A. Noll, *Christianity Today*

'A remarkably stimulating and helpful book.'

D. Clair Davis, *Evangelicals Now*

PENTECOST – TODAY?
*The Biblical Basis for
Understanding Revival*

ISBN 0 85151 752 8
234 pp., cloth-bound

'Many Christians are excited about the prospect of revival but little attention has been given to understanding its biblical basis . . . In this context Iain Murray's book must be welcomed . . . This is a hugely interesting work and one which is a necessary corrective to the superficial views and empty claims of much modern revivalism. Its grasp of theology and of history would enrich anyone's understanding of revival and all concerned with the issue ought to engage with what he has written. '

Theological Book Review

'Although I differ from the author at a number of points in his theology of the Holy Spirit, I hope profoundly that this new book is read by many of my fellow charismatics, for there is much wisdom and depth here that is badly needed in the circles I now move in . . . If you are a church leader you owe it to your people to read this sober assessment of where we are today, whatever your theological position.'

CLC Reviews of Books

Other booklets in this series from
The Banner of Truth Trust:

For details of other helpful publications and
free illustrated catalogue please write to

THE BANNER OF TRUTH TRUST

3 Murrayfield Road,   P O Box 621, Carlisle,
Edinburgh EH12 6EL   Pennsylvania 17013,
UK   USA

www.banneroftruth.co.uk